SELF-PORTRAIT BY AN OPEN WINDOW IN JUNE

Molly Andes

Copyright © 2021 by Molly Frances Andes

ISBN-13: 978-0-578-83978-3

Cover Design by Nana Nakazwe
@nn_frame18 on Instagram

DEAR READER

This book was born from the worst time of my life. It exists because poetry heals. When my body started falling apart, I found comfort and relief in writing these poems. If you suffer from chronic pain, I see you. I am with you. In the safety of these pages, I stopped trying to silver line mine and let it walk around bare. It made me feel better and I hope it makes you feel less alone. Pain is pain. Healing is healing.

Your self-portrait is beautiful. Hang it where you can see it.

TABLE OF CONTENTS

SELF-PORTRAIT BY A LILAC BUSH IN BLOOM   8

SELF-PORTRAIT BY AN OPEN WINDOW IN JUNE   16

SELF-PORTRAIT BY A PURPLE SEA AT DAWN   24

SELF-PORTRAIT BY A GLOWING CANDLE IN NEED   32

SELF-PORTRAIT BY AN ORANGE BOTTLE AT BREAKFAST   40

SELF-PORTRAIT IN AN UNMADE BED ALL DAY   48

SELF-PORTRAIT BY A FRIDA KAHLO PAINTING IN PERSON   56

SELF-PORTRAIT BY A WINDY HARBOR BEFORE SUNDOWN   64

SELF-PORTRAIT IN A SMUDGED MIRROR BEFORE SUNRISE   72

For my mother,

who has loved me through all my seasons.

"I paint self-portraits because I am so often alone, because I am the person I know best."

Frida Kahlo

one

Self-Portrait by a Lilac Bush in Bloom

self-portrait by a lilac bush
in bloom
my mother is beautiful and
tired
like hummingbirds
unceasing
wings beating to love the flowers
soft
arms like water
lemon sun
I read somewhere that we cannot
create new faces
in dreams
how many versions of
myself have existed
in sleep?
like marionettes
wooden
and performing stiff-limbed
thick
mind like molasses
petals rain
there are fairies living in
the grass

Secret Garden

I wish to live in a secret garden
with walls of ivy and white flowers
by a clear stream
under a knowing moon
in a peace
I have not yet been afforded

Under World

Persephone was picking flowers
when the world split beneath her.

there is something to be said about
the grieving. the heavy bleeding.

the thorns in skin and suffering
in the stems and petals left behind.

Butterfly

the beginning feels like the end. you
pretend you are a butterfly with a broken

wing. on the mend. but ready to return to
summer sky when the healing is done.

mossy green rest. sugar water elixir. try
everything the garden promises will fix you.

and you will be good as new soon.
and the flowers will be glad to see you.

Sea Glass

eggs were for breakfast. I practiced holding my
breath in hotel swimming pools and standing on

my head against the wall. the clouds were blue-
berry. I scarred my knee on Pennsylvania

pavement and my blood raced like rain to my
ankle. my mother said I needed a butterfly stitch.

tuna sandwiches were for lunch. my father painted
mountains in my bedroom and my mother taught

me to ski down real ones. the clouds were rasp-
berry. I liked maraschino cherries and collecting

green sea glass and roller-skating all over the
kitchen. I felt immediate and ate olives before

dinner.

                        toast is for breakfast. I practice
holding my breath in doctor's office waiting

rooms and standing with a fire in my spine. the
clouds are innocent. thank God, I have a good arm

for it and the blood races like a current to the vials.
my mother says I need to take a deep breath.

leftovers are for lunch. my father paints a positive
picture and my mother teaches me to be proactive

and I am lost in the every single day of it. the clouds
are constant. I like fresh cherries and collecting

green afternoons and driving on the highway by
myself. I feel immediate and eat olives for

                                                              dinner.

Muse

with every stolen muscle
and each claimed bone
and all held breaths
your violations are inspiring
the creation of a body
you cannot touch
or take away

two

Self-Portrait by an Open Window in June

self-portrait by an open window
in June
the lilacs have lived and
died
like dragonflies
fleeting
and more reliable in memory
sweet
cheeks like apples
amber sky
you can kiss me if you forget
my name
tomorrow
we can remove the stones
from each other's
pockets
like lovers
relieving
and more immediate in moonlight
open
hands like hymnals
curtains swim
there are pirate ships in the
clouds

Wildflowers

We drive up to Vermont again and the trees
are thick with summer. There are blue wild-
flowers on the side of the road and occasional
cows grazing in sprawling fields. I keep my
mind outside the window and my skin.

Wellness

I tell my mother this is the worst I have ever
felt and my father chops fresh basil from the

plant outside. you can taste the difference. my
hair drips from the shower. they play for five

hours and Novak Djokovic is the Wimbledon
champion. google says you shouldn't run during

a flare. it is the hottest June in 140 years. I tell
my father the pasta is delicious. you can taste

the difference. he asks if I remembered to take
my supplements. cabin fever is real. I add the

same silver lining when my friends ask how I
feel and make another appointment with my

therapist. full-flavor weariness. you can taste
the difference. I never forget my medicine and

try not to tell my mother this is the worst it's
ever been. she was there in the outpatient lot

the day after Thanksgiving. I am only slightly
alarmed when my ears start ringing. my body

thinks breaking is the way to fix it and Roger
Federer takes second place. the silver plate.

you can taste the difference. time for bed.
avoidance is comforting till two am and then it

melts on the hardwood. shame is less a friend

and more a breath. always waiting in my chest.

when they encourage deep breathing, I worry
about releasing it. about people seeing it bloom

like smoke in the air. it is humid in here. I don't
know how the spiders in my ceiling got in and

they are chopping basil on the cooking channel
again. I try not to imagine biting my tongue and

the drawing of blood. you can taste the difference.
seven months and Rome is still burning. what you

learn in this hell. it seems wellness works better
for those who are well.

Lullabies

you have hope
I have lullabies
leaking
through clenched fists

Before

garden salads on a patio. thirty dollar
emerald ring. shine it for you and you

can wear it out. everywhere heat. the
crosswalk lights white and a harpist

makes the air taste beautiful. ice cream
palms. there are boats floating where

the grass ends. when you leave you
realize you did not try to save them for

rain. you would have before. there are
careless clouds. scenic ride home. it

hurts to sleep and walk tomorrow. you
realize it is all rain. it wasn't before.

Siren

loneliness is the siren in me
and she puts out the call
but rocky shoreline surrounds
my heart
and you will find only
shipwreck here

three

Self-Portrait by a Purple Sea at Dawn

self-portrait by a purple sea
at dawn
blackberry stains on lips and
fingertips
like ink
temporary
and earned in the act
wet
feet like fish
bury me here and come
back for me
tomorrow
twenty-two seems awfully young
for pain but astrology
is becoming reasonable
like algebra
logical
and comforting in absolutes
new
heart like an oyster
opal water
there are mermaids walking on
the land

Island

I catch my breath in the middle of the ocean
my body is an island
I have not been able to swim
ashore

Lonely

these days the loneliness is an extra layer of
skin. it bruises easily and tightens when I try

to take deep breaths. it avoids sharp objects.
determined to protect the bones and breath

inside. terrified of bleeding out. but the extra
weight is heavy and the pressure applied is

steady and it is so busy locking you out, it
neglects the bleeding it is keeping in.

Surface

the cord of my throat is anchoring some monstrous
boat to this shallow spot in the ocean and I think,

somewhere on the surface, there is birdsong.

the sea is doing her best to wring my neck and slice
shards of sand through the skin of my legs and I think,

somewhere on the surface, there is sunlight.

I press flat palms to the shells of my ears and shelter
beneath shadows of passing sharks and eels and I think,

somewhere below the surface,
this is how people go mad.

Retrograde

I am aware of the lining of my skull. the
pink of my brain. she pulses all day and

asks silly questions. *what's for breakfast?
how does breathing feel today?* mercury

is merciless. flesh wounds don't heal in
the summer and the cantaloupe is going

bad on the counter. *what's for dinner?
do you think bones are supposed to feel

this way?* cold shower Saturday and early
to bed. the apples are red and dad bought

the purples olives I like. *do you think
Orion will be visible tonight? why aren't

you hungry?* sticky soda can sweat. we
can catch lightning bugs at eight forty

five pm. migraine mentality. pry open my
mouth and dust off the rafters. I've been

holding a scream in my throat like small
children hold caterpillars. with care. in no

rush to let go. *where did you go? how far
to the beach?* put the day under a pillow

and turn the fan on. the stars are all wrong
and the moon is a stone in my hands. sour

dreams and thirsty plants. crack open my

chest. spinal sadness. a fly has drowned in

my water glass. I watch it float for a while
and contemplate madness when I cannot

stop crying and I cannot stop laughing. *what
is for me? are you sick of eating toast?* the

day is dripping gold. liquid sun. I was
told more than once to wait for the good

part. museum art. fresh cherries by the sea
and the new grass in spring. in the swelling

thing behind my eyes I don't want to be
afraid. common side effects of retrograde.

Purge

I wake up in the shallows
slowly
the world is a blurry bright thing
the clouds let morning light in
I realize in my fingertips
my eyes are dripping
metal

four

Self-Portrait by a Glowing Candle in Need

self-portrait by a glowing candle
in need
my resolve is cracked and
peeling
like wallpaper
weathered
and revealing hidden walls
white
knuckles like knots
I want so badly to be touched
but my body hurts
at the slightest
I do not remember when
my skin stopped
being skin
like an eggshell
pale
and always at risk of breaking
quiet
face like marble
bitter air
there are monsters crawling into
the bed

Blackbirds

I have been laying in the wreckage
watching blackbirds soar
in the blue fabric
above me
waiting for a hand to appear

Cathedral

have you been biting down? glass teeth show
what's inside. the tongue is tied. no pews to

hide the people. a cherry-stained window of
a cracked smile cathedral. let them in. *where*

have you been? light candles for the dead. there
is a flicker at the back of the throat but it will

be extinguished by the breath. the living sin.
have you been sinking in? dark water drowns

dry land. no man's. the fish are taking flight.
catastrophe baptism in splinters of broken sky.

the tongues are tied. we all fall down. *can you
pull back flesh and be bloody now?* the bones

can hardly wait. fight to keep them off display
and mouth full of shards. and gasping for light.

Lungs

I am a museum of tired bones. a haunted
house with the lights on and the front door

wide open. you cannot see the whites of
my eyes. my skin is sticky and hot with

invisible blood. and I don't very much care
for mushrooms. the days grow like children.

my lungs are orange and I count on them to
sing me to sleep. you cannot see the burning

inside. the nights fog like glass. and it is
getting bad again. I pluck holy leaves and pray.

Survival Instinct

I am reaching new
valleys
and craters
and hollows
and I do not know if I will be able to continue on
but I always continue on
not
out of grit
or bravery
or perseverance
but out of a sort of numbness
that those who do not know any better
will call survival instinct

Still Life

lunchtime. I sit and cry on the kitchen floor and
think it will make a very bad poem. orange paint

on my fingers. the dogs like classical music. I
am tired of scrolling through rheumatologists

and you don't want to see your kids suffer on
your birthday. August breaks. I am a fixture of

the garden and not very good at reading tea
leaves. they always spell disaster to me. but

we have been watching the U.S. Open. you tell
me you knew all the players once and I begin

to understand why you love it so much. September
comes clean and on time. he cannot drink on his

21st so we play hangman at the table and eat
until the popcorn is gone. the dogs do not like

thunder. I am a muscle and an exposed Achilles
heel. the tremor is still in my fingers. dinner.

five

Self-Portrait by an Orange Bottle at Breakfast

self-portrait by an orange bottle
at breakfast
this is in control and
out
like falling
helpless
and at the mercy of the gods
weak
bones like fossils
unscrew the cap and
ignore the chills
and swallow
the healing will only
arrive if you invite
it inside
like a guest
unfamiliar
and waiting to be introduced
stubborn
will like a current
saltwater cure
there are griffins flying near
the sun

Yellow

My mother used to cut my hair in the kitchen and my bedroom didn't have any mirrors. I never knew that my bangs were uneven and breathed in without a fear of running out.

Ornament

this capsule is numbing. my skin is flaking off
and my hair collects at my feet like pine needles

from the Christmas tree we won't have this year.
my mother prefers the plastic kind from a box. it

is low maintenance. I am not low maintenance.
these nightmares are real. my lips are chewed

raw and my body is fragile like the ornaments
that stay in the box. too breakable for the branches.

Prayer

    nothing

            nothing

      nothing
nothing

             nothing

          nothing
              nothing

   nothing

        nothing
             nothing

   nothing

falls like sharp rainwater
into open palms
the only prayer
that remains

Name

I can feel the hunger in my throat and the
tape plays over and over. the tape plays

over and over. the tape plays over and
over. stacked. my voice is a whisper

and the circles are black and the oven
is on but it needs to be fixed. we haven't

baked anything in a year. lungs. I can
feel the bruising and the trees snag in

my ribs. the trees snag in my ribs. the
trees snag in my ribs. I am made up of

left behind leaves and best intentions to
breathe and I have no name anymore.

Degrees

I only let on small burnings. conceal
the forest fire. hide the flames behind

my back like a smoldering bouquet.
wilting shadows cast on my face.

I pretend the glow is healthy. smile
with all my teeth. bathe in icy water.

avoid puddles of gasoline. and pray
smoke doesn't scare you away.

six

Self-Portrait in an Unmade Bed All Day

self-portrait in an unmade bed
all day
someone is cutting their grass and
hedges
like split ends
unkempt
and unpleasant to look at
bitter
tongue like tightrope
call out of work and
lay down flat till
it subsides
turn on the cooking channel
your friend is engaged
and you are happy
like a fever
unsustainable
and waiting to break
tired
breath like burden
teardrop prayer
there is a phoenix weeping at
the window

Grace

I have been listening to the wind
pressing my ear up to the sky
hearing the familiar howl
and waiting
for you to replace it
but I have not been living
in the place where grace is

Nothing

I tell my mother I have nothing in me anymore and
she looks at me from across the kitchen. green tile

ocean. I cry out loud and the dogs sit in front of the
fan. I have been trying to even out my tan and keep

breathing recycled air. we both cradle the feeling
that this is not fair and corn on the cob boils in a pot.

once I start breaking I cannot stop and I don't want
to be this type of daughter. I look at my hands a lot

these days. just in case they are beginning to change.
every day I am more and more afraid of the body I am

inhabiting. war within skin. she tells me it sounds like
depression. I don't know how to explain this is worse.

Avoidance

this page is too quiet
too empty
too breathless
and I am too bursting
too ravaged
too weary
to close the gap today

Mantra

sit in the sun and bite through an apple
sky thick September blue
deliberate jaw
orange sun through closed lashes
it's okay
it's okay
it is okay

say it over and over until it bleeds through the
I don't believe you

Seasons

if you knew me before
you knew an orange
unpeeled and a
lily pad drowning
in fresh water
if you knew me in the middle
you knew a blind
hurricane and a
sandcastle built
in the ocean
if you know me tomorrow
you know ten rows
of teeth and why
soft things survive
long winters

seven

Self-Portrait by a Frida Kahlo Painting in Person

self-portrait by a Frida Kahlo painting
in person
there are moments in color and
ache
like flashes
surreal
and most beautiful in their brevity
clear
eyes like mirrors
I see the thorns around your
neck and feel them
pierce my own
this is the ugly and why I
love you and why I
cling to you
like a mother
warm
and wiser from pain before me
tough
ribs like armor
summer fruit
there are angels painting in
the sky

Ache

the goddesses before you
must have felt it too
when they were chiseled
from marble
to art

Retrograde Reprisal

the trees are red through the exam room window
and people are driving to work. white crinkle

paper clean. *have you been exercising and how
is your sleep?* my mother takes slippery ink notes

and I squeeze ten fingers around the frog in my
throat until I hope the life has gone out. press into

the triggers and assess joints. evaluate tongue and
listen to lung noise. *where does it hurt in a body*

that burns? revoke the answers before and don't
provide any more. pick a tree and pray not to croak.

where is hope?

Gazers

We sat in a lawn chair in the backyard and talked about young things. I was still small enough for her lap and she was still bigger than my cuts and scrapes. I rose with my mother's breathing and dangled my feet above early September grass. She adjusted the blanket and I shifted my weight and we both pretended to know what we were looking at. If I was sore, it was soreness I'd earned. And it melted in sleep. I don't remember a body that worked. But I can still taste the cool hush of stars. Still make myself small and place myself back in her arms. It is blinding. The relief to be her daughter.

Exhibit

this is where it settles. I sleep with three pillows
and one eye open. my bedroom is an aquarium

and most days I lay at the bottom of the tank. the
canvas is blank but I collect bottles of paint and

new symptoms. my arms are full of bruised apples
and I spend hours cleaning the dust out from under

my bed. my fingers catch on coral and blood in the
water is normal but sometimes people tap on the

glass. I am not a forgotten exhibit because people
still tap on the glass. I want to thank you for that.

Hope

I painted you on the inside of my ribcage
so every time my heart grew weary
it could see why it was beating

eight

Self-Portrait by a Windy Harbor Before Sundown

self-portrait by a windy harbor
before sundown
the water is alive and
glistening
like canvas
wet
and freshly painted by the sun
warm
skin like salt
take the ship out of the
bottle and place the
peaceful in it
carry it with you for
the days the pain
is winning
like a talisman
personal
and offering protection
surrender
body like island
ruthless waves
there are nymphs singing on
the shore

Ceremony

dizzy spells are inevitable
and the bleeding is to be expected
but you can patch up my chest
with fallen
oranges and reds
when the sky is slate and stony
divine
autumnal ceremony

Bath

I soaked myself in a lukewarm bath and held my breath above water. Weightless bubbles glinted in heaps around my knees and trailed lazily up to my chin. I traced the weathered tap with my big toe and looked down at myself from somewhere else. Pale cream nail polish chipping. Steady cold stream dripping into the tub and leaching the heat from the bath. I watched it all far away. Glad not to be soup in that water.

Bird

the frost knows who she's claiming. have you seen
a bird with snow for wings? the bloodwork on

Monday should give us answers.

I apply honey to my skin and you bathe in
cinnamon maybe sweeter things will come if

we decide them.

I
don't believe it but for you I know I'm trying.

November bares her teeth. have you seen
a bird shed all her feathers? the X-ray on

Tuesday should give us answers.

you find fresh water in a desert and I am barely
tethered maybe healing things will come if

we invite them.

I
don't believe it but for you I know I'm trying.

winter waits for me. have you seen a bird
made of wind and rain? the colonoscopy on

Thursday should give us answers.

I choke on sentiment and you fashion me a
splint maybe warmer things will come if

we insist them.

I
don't believe it but for you I know I'm trying.

have you seen a bird on the side of the road?
feathers stripped, bone on bone. the MRI on

Friday should give us answers.

I hold salt in empty palms and you drive with
quiet calm maybe there are no answers

and this is it.

I
don't believe it but for you I know I'm trying.

December

I sat in a snowbank and let my lipstick melt
all of my years in my bones
you held my breath
and I watched yours bloom
and we both tried not to freeze through

Apricot Jam

the sky is thick with unshed snow. opal
ceiling. I play my mother's old records

and cut eight inches of my hair. Sylvia
Plath God rest her soul. we hang star-

shaped lights and hope the next twelve
months are better. Father Doyle tells

me Cape Bretton would be a beautiful
place to write poetry and my mother

cannot stop rearranging decorations. I
wish I could shower off the ache. soap

healing. I start putting apricot jam on
my toast and dance in front of the mirror.

the grass begins to swallow the snow.
Father Doyle God rest his soul.

nine

Self-Portrait in a Smudged Mirror Before Sunrise

self-portrait in a smudged mirror
before sunrise
I am beautiful and
tired
like honeybees
searching
unearthing nectar from the thousandth flower
weep
soul like stream
I read somewhere that you would not
recognize yourself if you
walked past you
my features are so changed by ache
there is a stranger in the glass
in my bedroom
like me
soft
but harsher and fraying at the edges
lost
mind like maelstrom
constellation plea
there are goddesses arriving on
the moon

New Peace

I do not live in a secret garden
with walls of ivy and white flowers
I live in pain
under a knowing moon
in a war
I am coming to accept as peace

Eulogy

cut all my hair and
build a bird's nest
my teeth will not matter
someday
my ribs
will be fossils buried
beneath the roots of
dandelions
and the sun will fry
worms on cracked
dirt
I will be
remembered
by no one
and every cloud
I ever counted

Flamingos

The sky is flushed. Blushing through the raindrops
on my windshield. It makes me breathe in color. I
remember a documentary I watched once about
flamingos. They flocked to an African salt pan when
it was suddenly flooded to mate. By the time their
babies were born it was a scalding climate again.
David Attenborough said the journey to fresh water
could take 50 kilometers. Survival of the fittest.
A little flamingo baby was left behind with salt
solidifying around his ankles. My eyes are clear
in the rearview mirror and the sky has paled
after rain.

Peonies

I planted peonies in my right shoulder blade
they bloom all year round
a gentle reminder
that even the softest things
can grow from
bone

Honey Hi

I wake up and play Tusk all the way
through. yellow flowers absolute in

a vase. green legs vulnerable through
the glass. 23 for 7 days and every poem

I have written feels like a poem of the
past. I know it is mine. I breathe and

the sun touches each roof slat of the
house across the street. naked yesterday

words on the page. blinking exposed in
the light. I thank them for keeping me alive.

ACKNOWLEDGEMENTS

I am anchored by good people. My "thank you's" could fill this book and replace the poems. I'll be forever grateful for the friends and family who have supported me and offered comfort during this period of change. Chronic pain is lonely. You've gotten in its way.

This book was a way for me to get in its way, too.

The beautiful cover design would not have been possible without my wonderful friend Nana Nakazwe. Thank you, Nana. You've made my childhood dream a reality and it is so much better than I could have imagined.

This collection scared me for a long time and I wasn't sure if I would ever be ready to share it. My friend Keith Dooley received my words without judgement and empowered me as a writer. Thank you, Keith, I'm so grateful for your insights and compassion.

These pages are full because people encouraged me.

Thank you, Veronica, for checking in and making me laugh and always understanding. I would be lost without your detailed superstitions and generous belief in me.

Thank you, Jaye, for listening and always lifting me up. You saw this in me at sixteen when I could barely see the next day. These poems are honest and breathing because of you.

Thank you, Steve, for surrounding me with love. Your constant support has meant everything. I am brighter and better for knowing and loving you.

My family have nurtured me and my writing my entire life.

Thank you, Honey, for being the biggest cheerleader in my life. You have only ever encouraged me to be myself and that's an incredible gift.

Thank you, Grandma, for sharing your stories and your books and your time with me. I will know I have made it when one of my books earns a spot on your coffee table.

Thank you, Matthew, for being an example of strength to me every day. I am grateful and proud to be your sister.

Thank you, Dad, for telling me about nutrition books you've read and accommodating my ever-changing dietary needs. You are a steady, reassuring presence in my life.

Thank you, Mom, for taking notes in doctor's offices and never giving up. You endure every day of pain with me and still remind me there is light.

Finally, I want to thank the Chronic Illness community. Your honesty and vulnerability made me feel seen at a time when I felt most invisible and alone. I didn't know resilience until I discovered all of you.

Pain is an isolating thing and writing is often a solitary activity. The process was messy and healing and done alone.

The sharing is with you and it's freeing.

Thank you for reading.

Find more of my poetry on Instagram

@mfapoetry

Get in touch with me

mollyfa1815@gmail.com

www.ingramcontent.com/pod-product-compliance
Lightning Source LLC
Chambersburg PA
CBHW070629050426
42450CB00011B/3147